THE
GIFT

Stories about my brother for his children...

By Marianne Duffill Cox

ISBN-13: 978-1548351922
ISBN-10: 154835192X

Book Design
Donna Overall
donnaoverall@bellsouth.net

Photographs and Memories
Members of the Evans and Alexander families

My sincere thanks to Lea Hinson, Alan Rachels, Ronald Rachels, Tom Newton, Ellen Fuller, Charlie Roy Hall, Roslyn Martin, Rusty Foster, and Delilah Alexander.

Other Books by Marianne Duffill Cox
Troubadour of the Troubled
Living Consciously

Marietta, Georgia

TABLE OF CONTENTS

About the Author

Marianne Cox is an avid writer who lives in Marietta, Georgia. She is retired from nursing and managing rental property. This is her third book, and she is now working on a fourth and fifth book, so look for them in the future.

Her fourth book will be about her many trips around the world. She has been traveling most of her life, from Alaska to Argentina and Iceland, to China and New Zealand. A trip to Antarctica is in the works for this winter.

Her fifth book will be another book of essays, which she has also started working on. She isn't sure what the sixth book will be about yet, but she loves writing and feels the inspiration will come.

INTRODUCTION

It came to me late one night, as I lay in bed trying to go to sleep. I had been thinking about family a lot and wishing we could spend more time together and know each other better. There has been this huge empty space I have felt all my life. What would it have been like to have a father and how would it have made my life different? I will never know, because my father died when I was only ten months old, and all the people that could tell me about him are gone.

But, I thought, this doesn't have to happen to Hugh's children. Even though all of his children were very young when he died, there are still lots of people around to tell his stories. I decided I would make it my mission to gather my brother's stories for his children and future generations so they could know him.

This project began in January of 2016. The first step was to collect as many stories from as many people as possible. I didn't anticipate that this would be the most difficult part of the project. It seems getting people to write and email you even a short piece is like asking them to write a term paper. Doing interviews seems to be easier for them. It took about a year and a half to collect all the stories and information for the book.

Several of the key people that were Hugh's best friends have already left us, such as Don Goodson and Michael Morris. I was not able to reach others, such as Jim Houser and John Maben. I gathered as many stories as I could in the year and a half that I was doing this, and I learned a lot about Hugh myself.

As you will find out as you read, Hugh really loved his family—his siblings, his cousins, his aunts, his grandmother, his wife, and his children. He made time for the people in his life that he cared about, and that was family and friends.

Some people might have thought that Hugh lived his life in a rather reckless way because he tended to do dangerous things, like skydiving and air racing. I believe that he lived fearlessly and that living without fear was the only way he knew how to live. He lived life to the fullest and experienced life to the fullest. Not all of us are strong enough to do that. Maybe that's why so many people admire him and love him. He was able to live his life in a way that most of us could only dream of.

My hope is that this book will give Hugh's children and grandchildren some insight into who he was. I also hope that the book will be passed down for generations so that the great grandchildren will also know him. I wish there was such a book about my past relatives, especially such an interesting and colorful person as Hugh.

CHAPTER ONE

Family Background

Although my book is about Hugh Causey Alexander, Jr., born June 12, 1942, I want to give you some family background history. The first Alexanders came to America in 1774 from Ireland on a ship named "Hopewell," and they were given a land grant from the King of England for some land in Georgia.

Jumping forward a hundred years or so, I want to talk about John David Hugh Alexander, who was the grandfather of my subject, Hugh Alexander, Junior. John David Alexander married twice and had children by both wives. The first wife was Margret Adela Fleming and their children were Hugh Bothwell Alexander and James Fleming Alexander. James is the grandfather of Rosalyn, Jimmy, and Ann

John David Alexander

LouEllen Johnson

Alexander, who were second cousins to my subject, Hugh.

John David's second wife was LouEllen Johnson from "Shakerag," or later known as Wadley, Georgia. They had five boys and one girl, Billy, Pressley, Julian, Harvey, Causey, and Sara. The girl died at five years old.

The house that Hugh Causey Alexander, Senior, grew up in was built by his father, John David, in 1918. This house is still in excellent shape because it has been kept in the family and has been lived in continuously. I visited the house in 2017 and took this picture.

The house Causey grew up in.

John David not only was a farmer but he also delivered mail. Causey lived there until he was twenty two years old. A couple of the other brothers also stayed home into their twenties. I guess it was just too convenient having mother cook and clean for them.

When they did finally get kicked out and on their own, they all did exceedingly well. Causey and Julian became farmers near home, Harvey had a hardware store in Brookhaven in Atlanta, Pressley raised cattle near Louisville, Georgia, and Billy worked for a realtor in Atlanta before moving back home to become a farmer.

Annie Cecil Evans met Causey, Hugh's father, when she was working at a seed and feed store in Louisville, Georgia. He came in to buy some seed several times and eventually asked her out on a date. After the courtship, they married in January, 1937. The first few

Bothwell, Pressley, Ralph, Harvey, Billy, and Causey Alexander

years, they lived in a small house outside Louisville, where their first three children were born.

Causey and Annie moved to Magruder Farm on November 3, 1942, when Hugh was only five months old. The farm was a little over 6,200 acres or about ten square miles. The house at Magruder was also large. It had a huge living room, 72 feet long by 20 feet wide. Alongside the living room were three large bedrooms with one bathroom. Across the front of the house was a full screened in porch. In the back of the house, there was the dining room, the breakfast room, the kitchen, and another bedroom. All

The house at Magruder Farm

this was upstairs, and downstairs there was a store Causey ran.

Our father was not only a farmer, but he was also a sales representative for International Harvester, which sells farm equipment. He specifically sold Farmall tractors. Causey got his pilot's license and plane so he could fly to meetings for the

Causey and his plane.

company to make sales. He had a grass landing strip at Magruder near the house with his plane parked there. The same flight instructor that taught Causey to fly later gave his son Hugh flying lessons.

Causey was a very good business man as well as a good farmer. At one time, Magruder was the biggest farm in Georgia. He was the first farmer in Georgia to buy a cotton picker, and there was an article in the magazine section of the Atlanta paper about this. *(See pages 5-8)* Cotton was being picked by hand, which was very slow, and the new machine was much faster. Causey was also the first farmer in South Georgia to plant soybeans and make it a profitable crop. His neighbors thought he was crazy when he first did it, but when they saw him making profit, they started planting soybeans too.

After our mother's father died, and the Wadley Bank needed help, because he had been the president of the bank, the major stockholder, and it needed direction after his death, Causey bought the stock. Things did stabilize, and my father held the stock and left it to my mother. She continued to hold it, because her husband told her to never sell it. In the end, its value increased substantially, thanks to my father's good advice to my mother. *(Continued on page 9)*

Hugh Causey Alexander, Senior

Belle Dickey, who lives in the house in the background, drives the new **cotton picker** on H. C. Alexander's plantation at Magruder, Ga.

Cotton Picker ON WHEELS

By Willard Neal

JOURNAL COLOR PHOTOS
BY HAROLD J. TEBRUNE

Girls from Waynesboro and from nearby farms climbed aboard the cotton picker for a ride. The machine could pick twice as fast as all of them working together.

PICKING COTTON, a job that Southern farmers hardly hoped to get out of this side of heaven, now is being taken over by machinery.

The new picker literally eats up the rows of cotton, moving at a good fast trot and roaring like a million bumble bees. After it has passed, the stalks stand up as straight as ever, hardly disturbed by the going-over they have had, but robbed of their snowy locks as cleanly as if picked by field hands.

And the cotton drops into the huge hopper atop the machine as clean and free of leaves as human hands would pick it.

In other words, the mechanical cotton picker is a success, or at least that was the opinion of a group of farmers who watched a demonstration on H. C. Alexander's farm at Magruder near Waynesboro in Burke County.

Mr. Alexander has just bought an International Harvester model, the second one in Georgia, to pick the 500 acres of cotton on his 6,295-acre plantation, and the neighbors had come over to see its first workout. Among the observers were a lot of schoolgirls, who had picked quite a bit of cotton by the stoop-and-fumble method simply because they thought it was the patriotic thing to do, and they broke out in cheers when the machine started picking more cotton in a minute than they could in an hour.

The new picker looks like a short-coupled betsy bug, painted red, and carrying a huge cotton basket on its back. The business end is just inside its mouth. The picking is done by 600

bright steel spindles, similar to those of a textile mill, which whirl at high speed Each spindle has a row of needle-like protuberances, to catch the fibers and wind the cotton up on the spindle.

The spindles are mounted in rows a little over an inch apart, and operate from a drum which turns backward at the same speed the machine moves forward, so that the whirling spindles actually are stationary in the stalk, just as the bottom of an automobile tire is always standing still on the ground, regardless of how fast the car may be moving.

The cotton picker goes roaring down the row, taking the stalks into its big mouth and bending the outer limbs inward, so that the rows of spindles can slide in from each side and snatch out the cotton. After the spindles turn back inside the machine the cotton is brushed off by rubber buffers and thrown into a suction chute which sends it upstairs to the waiting basket.

There had been a cloudburst the night before, and the cotton in the bolls was soggy wet. Mr. Alexander did not plan to do much picking until it dried, but he considered that an excellent chance to try out the machine under adverse conditions. And the machine went right ahead as if it were working under ideal circumstances.

Expert cotton growers, following along the rows, commented on the fact that stalks were not broken, and they failed to find where a single unopened boll had been knocked off or damaged. Everyone commented on how little trash was picked with the cotton. This cleanliness was due partly to advance preparations made by Mr. Alexander.

"While the machine was being assembled, I dusted the fields with cyanamid, a very strong nitrate fertilizer," Mr. Alexander explained. "This caused all the

Picking cotton the old way, for the last time, are Mary Stone, Joan Rogers and Grace Crocket (left to right), of nearby Waynesboro, Ga.

Cotton from the machine is as clean as human hands could pick it, say Gwen Netherland, Carolyn Mobley and Ruth Watford (left to right).

J. L. Pennington, farm superintendent, watching cotton pour into the truck, said the picker solves one of the farmer's biggest problems.

leaves to fall off. I've been doing this several years, and found it worth the cost and trouble for a number of reasons. When the leaves drop, the sun can get in, which drives boll weevils to the shade of the woods. The sun also causes the bolls to open immediately, so that one or two pickings will get all the cotton, and there are no dried leaves to stick to the cotton as it is being picked. The cyanimid falls to the ground with the leaves, and since it is a fertilizer that doesn't leach rapidly, it remains in the soil to help grow the next year's crop."

Mr. Alexander appeared well pleased with his machine. In fact, he seemed as happy as a youngster with a new toy.

"It does everything the salesman said it would," he declared. "I've done a little figuring on costs, and it looks like a bargain, too. Manual pickers are charging $1.50 to $2.25 a hundred pounds. At $1.60 a hundred, the cost amounts to $20 a bale.

"This machine cost $4,900, so it will

pay for itself with the first 240 bales it picks. We have 500 acres, and should get about three-quarters of a bale to the acre. The cost of hiring our fields picked would amount to more than the original price of the machine plus operational expenses."

J. H. Reese, who has 300 acres of cotton near Waynesboro, watched the picker moving up and down the rows, eating up the cotton as busily as an army worm. "That's the thing we've all been waiting for," he said. "I've raised cotton 30 years, and every year when I plant it, I start worrying over whether I'll ever get it all picked."

The kids had their own ideas about the cotton field robot, too. When we first saw the picker it was being driven by Belle Dickey, high school-age daughter of a supervisor on the plantation. She was sitting on the high poop deck and leaning far over the steering wheel as she watched the cotton row disappear into the mouth of the big red picker.

"It's hard to guide at first," she said. "You see it has three wheels, and steers by the rear one, so you catch yourself over-steering, the way you do driving an automobile backward. But running the machine, even for a beginner, is easier than bending over a cottonstalk to get those bottom bolls—or hugging a heavy picksack that is almost full. On that high seat the briars can't scratch your ankles, either. Life on the farm is going to be lots more fun when you can look at growing cotton and not have that sinking feeling that someday you've got to pick it."

Paul Jones, a company representative from Atlanta, was on hand to train the new operators, and he gave some of the machine's history.

"We've been working on the cotton picker about 30 years, and just now have it developed well enough to market," he said. "Those 30 years saw a lot of brilliant achievements and a lot of heartbreaks. Every summer our Cotton Cara-

van started at Brownsville, Texas, in July, and ended up in Arkansas around Christmas, picking cotton free just for the chance to try out the machines.

"Inventors, mechanics and tool shops went along, so that repairs could be made, and new ideas tried out, on the spot. During the spring the machines were taken apart and rebuilt, always with the aim of picking all the cotton, getting it clean, and doing the job fast.

"As far as we can tell, the machine now is complete. It is geared to cover an acre and a half in one hour and 15 minutes, regardless of whether the cotton is thick or poor—the only difference to the picker is that you have to unload when the hopper is filled with 750 pounds of cotton."

The picker went roaring down another row, and every shoulder in the field seemed to straighten a little, as the observers realized there would be no more bending over the cotton stalks.

.ug. 26, 1945

ly

ne

of Burke
is part of
d machine
Negroes.

gro would
machine
.

the ma-
with the
unty, but
ster peo-
er, have
om east-
the ma-
he open
er farm-
ether to
achine.
ill buy
avail-
a small
watch-

dville,
iruder
buy
t was
bar-
rank
ckett,

Constitution Staff Photos—Kenneth Rogers

REVOLUTION IN THE COTTON PATCH—The big red cotton picker in Burke county that looks like a cement mixer might revolutionize Georgia's principal crop. Since
it's capable of picking between seven and eight bales a day, cotton farmers around

Just up the dirt road from Boiling Springs, on Causey's Magruder farm, was the "Alexander Crossroads." At this crossroads, each direction led to an Alexander farm. Coming from Boiling Springs, on Eden Church Road, if you turned right, you went to Uncle Billy's farm; if you turned left, you went to Uncle Pressley's farm; and if you went straight, you went to Ralph's farm.

Of course, on the road you were coming from was Causey's farm. Billy had married Aunt Minnie, and they had moved to her family farm, where they hired an overseer to manage it for them. Pressley had bought Old Town Plantation and was raising cattle.

When Hugh was old enough to start walking, Causey had a play yard made for the kids. The fence was made out of chicken wire. It was behind the house, and there was a sand box and some trees. There was one tree that was so close to the fence that the older kids could climb the tree and escape. Hugh was too small to get out, and he was the main one meant to be kept in, but he wasn't very happy when they got out and left him.

With so many children, there was lots of help. Aunt Sissy, the babysitter, and Sook, the cook, were full time help. Mary Pennington was a nurse that came whenever she was needed and sometimes stayed for weeks at a time.

Nurse Mary Pennington

Aunt Sissy

Sook

During World War II, probably around 1944 or 1945, German prisoners of war were brought here; some lived at Uncle Pressley's farm, Old Town. They would work on farms in the area, Magruder included. Lou Ellen, Causey's oldest daughter, remembers handing out cigarettes to them. Causey sold Bermuda grass to the military during the war. They used it to plant grass to make new grass landing strips for temporary air fields.

Causey and Annie had two more children after they moved to Magruder. Sara was born on March 19, 1945, and I, Marianne, was born on January 10, 1948. I was born at home in the house at Magruder. Mary Pennington, the nurse, was there, and Dr. Peacock was called. When the doctor got there, the family pet goat wouldn't let him up the stairs. By the time he finally got in the house, I was already born. I've been told that Hugh wouldn't look at me for days. He was mad because I wasn't a boy.

Magruder was a little over 6200 acres. Causey farmed about 2000 acres, and the rest was in lumber, which was cut for profit ever so often. The overseer of the farm was Laurence Pennington, who lived with his family right around the corner from our family.

Our father had many employed workers on the farm to do all sorts of work. They made cement blocks and then built houses out of them for some of the workers to live in. When the phone company couldn't provide service to the farm from Louisville, they cut and creosoted poles, and constructed the lines themselves, all done with farm workers and farm materials. It was a four party line, but at least they had phone service, thanks to Causey.

Causey was a very progressive farmer for his time. He was an early user of aerial crop dusting. He had a fully equipped maintenance garage and mechanics to keep all the farm equipment running. Those block houses he built were permanent housing for his workers that need a place to live, and his workshop built accessories like front-end loaders and blades attachments.

Every Summer, Causey would have a big barbecue for all his employees. They would cook a whole pig, and the ladies would bring all the side dishes. Everybody came—from the overseer and his family to Aunt Sissy, our babysitter, Sook, Annie's cook, the lowest man on the working totem pole, and Causey and all his family. It was a big event, and everyone had a great time.

CHAPTER TWO

Life on the Farm

Hugh's first ten years were spent at Magruder. What a great place for a young boy growing up. There were so many fun things to do. It was obvious Causey loved his children because he had every conceivable fun thing for them to play with in the yard. They had a seesaw, a swing, a sandbox, and a pony with a cart. Hugh had a little jeep, Lou Ellen had a horse, they had the swimming pool, a sliding board at the pool, and a raft, and they had Aunt Sissy to look after them. He did everything he could to give his children a safe and happy life.

Soon after moving to Magruder, Causey began working on building a swimming pool around Boiling Springs. When he finished the retaining walls for the pool, he had all the

Boiling Springs

Causey and Hugh

kids put their foot and hand prints on the top bracket of the cement which was spaced about every eight feet to stabilize the wall. Delilah, Hugh's wife, now has his cement footprint in her backyard in Decatur, Georgia.

The swimming pool we called Boiling Springs is just a couple of miles from the farm house. The natural spring in the middle of the pool was about twenty feet long and twelve feet wide. He made a large pool, about an acre, around it by building a concrete wall with a spillway at one end so you could control the level of the water in the pool. The water was crystal clear and had a sandy bottom at one end where the moss was kept cleared off. The water was very cold but felt great on a hot summer day. Lots of days were spent at the pool for picnics and swimming for many years.

There was a stream that had been there for a long time. That is where Causey had located the spillway for the pool, so the water could run out from the pool into the stream. The stream was used by Indians many years ago, and many arrowheads and pottery fragments were found by Hugh and the other children.

The stream was a favorite place to play because there were lots of vines big enough to swing on and play Tarzan. Also, Causey bought an old army surplus raft for them to play on. In the beginning it had a bottom made out of ropes lashed across back and forth. Later, when the ropes rotted, it was just a bottomless rectangle of floating sides, but it was still fun playing who could stay on the longest without getting pushed off.

Raft at Boiling Springs

There were a few eels that lived in the pool. They could hide in the moss, because only part of the sandy bottom of the pool was kept free of moss. Hugh told Ellen that one of the eels lived in the spring and if she wanted to see it, he knew how she could. He found a concrete block, a little smaller than the usual big ones, got an inner tube and tied a rope to it. One end of the rope was tied to the block, the other end was tied to the inner tube, and he told Ellen to get in the inner tube. He also made a harness out of rope for Ellen to put on and attached the other end of the

Hugh and Ellen with Nelly and the pony cart

rope to the block. If she slipped out of the inner tube, the cement block wouldn't take her down, according to Hugh, because the spring was so strong it would push her back up. She survived!

Besides the pool, there was a pony and cart for the children. The pony's name was Nelly. Hugh and his sisters could all pile in and go for a ride whenever they could get someone to

Fun on the swings.

Sara and Marianne.

Hugh and Major, the bird dog.

hook it up for them. That wasn't very hard to do with all the help around. There was also a horse named Polly, and another horse named Betsy that belonged to Jimmy, their cousin.

Many adventures were had in the woods behind the big house, where there was a teepee. It was made out of bare, long tree limbs, and the base was an old wagon wheel.

The pony and horses provided a way for Hugh and the kids to go off on their own for all kinds of fun excursions. Major, the bird dog, usually would come along to pull a travois, which is an Indian way of carrying things, with two sticks fastened to either side of the dog and the other ends of the sticks dragging the ground. With this, you fastened your load between the two sticks, so the dog could pull the load. They would be gone for the afternoon, snacks in hand, and not come home till they were called home by the car horn blowing.

Magruder was a big farm where a lot of cotton was grown, so there would be huge bales of cotton stacked up before they were carried off to be sold. Hugh and the kids would build a fort. There were always lots of kids around, especially in the summer. Cousins and friends were always coming to visit, because Magruder was such a fun place for kids. They would divide up and battles would be fought.

The cotton bales were stored in an area just behind the house. This being one of their favorite places, they thoughtlessly were playing with sparklers back there, and caught several bales on fire. Everyone got a spanking for that one. They could have caught the house on fire. As usual, Hugh was in the middle of the mischief.

One time, when they were playing, Hugh decided he would fix everyone some food. He told them he could cook it right there on the rocks; it was so hot. The flapjacks didn't work very well, but the scrambled eggs weren't too bad according to Ellen, his cousin.

Another favorite thing to do on the farm was to play on the tractor. It had a crane with a long chain hanging down from it with a big hook on the end. Hugh thought it would be fun to put a wash pan on the hook, sit one of the kids in the pan, and then he would turn the crank and haul them high up in the air. Ellen was the first to try it, and when Hugh got her up there, she was about six or seven feet above the ground. All of a sudden, Hugh let the brake off and Ellen

Lou Ellen and her horse.

Two-year-old Hugh with his jeep.

Hugh's cousin Ellen

The seesaw was a favorite.

There were several kinds of swings to play on.

Ellen

went screaming toward to the ground, only stopping short a few inches away.

If this sounds like an accident waiting to happen, you're right. Sara, Hugh's younger sister, decided to try the pan ride and was terrified before she even got to the top. Seeing this, Ellen tried to stop Hugh from letting her drop by grabbing the chain. It sliced her finger, and Hugh told her he would fix it with an aspirin and bandage it up. Ellen was afraid to tell her Aunt Annie because, the summer before, she had an accident sliding down the sliding board. It also involved Hugh. He had put a hose pipe at the top of the slide and run water down it so the kids could slide faster. Unfortunately, when Ellen went down the slide, there was a broken Coke bottle on the ground right where her foot landed. She had a big gash in the side of her foot, had to go to the doctor for stitches, and couldn't swim at Boiling Springs. Even though the finger didn't seem as bad as the foot, she was still afraid to tell Hugh's mom. The scar on her finger never went away.

Just down the road from the house was a huge sawdust pile. This was another fun place to play. You could climb to the top and slide to the bottom. On your way, as you walked over to it, you could see the bobcat that the neighbor had in a cage—so many fun things to do.

The big house at Magruder had this long, long living room with a fireplace and lots of room for kids to run around when it was cold outside.

Hugh on the sliding board

Another fun feature of the old house was the closets. These closets were built so that there were shelves on both sides that you could climb up to the top and crawl onto the flat shelf across the top of the closet where blankets were kept. This was a perfect place to hide.

This idealistic life wasn't to last forever. Causey was diagnosed with an inoperable brain tumor sometime in 1948, the same year I was

On the tractor.

born with serious medical problems. He was in the hospital in Augusta, Georgia at the same time I was in St. Joseph's Hospital in Atlanta. Annie was driving back and forth between the two cities. Our father died in November of 1948. I was just 10 months old; Lou Ellen, the oldest was only 10 years old.

CHAPTER THREE

Life in Wadley

Hugh loved the farm and what young boy wouldn't? He was only six years old when his father died. His mother managed to stay on the farm for four more years with five young children, but when Hugh was ten, the family was moved fourteen miles away to Wadley, Georgia. It was a big adjustment for a young boy that was used to having so much freedom and adventure that the farm had given him. The children couldn't take all their animal friends with them. Living in town was very different for all of them.

There were some vacant lots that ran behind all the houses from Grandma's, Uncle Bubba's, all the way down to Hugh's new house. This became the new place to play. In a

School Days
1948-49

field across the street from those vacant lots, there were some cows that the kids tried to milk once, but of course that didn't work.

There was a large deserted manual concrete mixer on one of the vacant lots. It had a big wheel that you could turn to make the barrel come down, so you could pour the concrete out. Hugh had the idea that it would be fun to put one of the kids in the barrel and roll it up. Of course it wouldn't be *him* that got in the barrel. He would be the one to be turning the wheel. This was the usual way with his ideas. Once they were in the barrel and it was turned up, he would let the wheel go so it would roll down and dump them out. This was fun the first time or two, then the older cousins, Hugh and Ellen, decided to put the younger ones in, roll them up, lock it in place, and leave them for a while so they couldn't get out. They couldn't even climb out because the same bar that locked the wheel was across the top of the opening of the barrel.

Living room in Wadley house.

Although he was very mischievous, Hugh also had a sweet side. He found time to play with his younger sisters. How many ten-year-olds are willing to spend time with a four-year-old sister and let them ride him like a horse all over the living room. Hugh would get down on all fours in his pee jays and let me, a four-year-old, ride and pretend he was my horse. There was a big living room in Wadley, so there was lots of space for this game.

SCHOOL DAYS 1951-52

Rusty Foster also recalls a time when, somehow, Hugh was talked into spending some time playing with him as a kid. Probably both their mothers were playing Bridge in Annie's living room at the time, or something, and Hugh was asked to look after Rusty. Anyway, Hugh had made a model airplane and when it was time for Rusty to go home, Hugh gave it to him. Rusty couldn't believe Hugh's generosity. As a teenager Rusty became a big Hugh fan and wanted to be just like Hugh.

The house in Wadley had a table for six in the kitchen. Annie sat at the head of the table, and Hugh, being the only male in the family, sat at the foot of the table. I, being the youngest, sat on one side, next to Annie, and Sara beside me, with Lou Ellen and Willa on the opposite side. The table was the same kitchen table from Magruder. It had been special made, probably in the store below the big house at the farm. The breakfast room in the house at the farm was very narrow, so that's why a custom table had to be made.

Things were never quiet at the Alexander house. Hugh got a set of drums for Christmas one year and set them up in the foyer of the living room. He

Kitchen in Wadley house.

The foyer.

had a band called "Alexander's Ragtime Band." Annie actually let them practice there. Hugh's band was in "Spring Frolics" that year.

Behind the house heading toward Foster's Pond, all the roads were dirt. It was a good place for young drivers to practice or do crazy stuff like make the car do fish tails. Lou Ellen and Hugh were going for a ride, and the family station wagon got in the ditch. Hugh had the job of walking to the nearest house for help. Turned out the nearest farmer with a tractor to pull them out was Mr. Goodson's place. Being a nice guy, and knowing the Alexander kids, Mr. Goodson agreed to

take his tractor and pull the car out. He just had one question for Hugh, "Is she drunk?" Hugh walked back to the car and told Lou Ellen, because he wasn't sure what Mr. Goodson meant, but Lou Ellen knew. He thought Annie was driving the car, and knew her reputation for having a few too many drinks. He showed up with his tractor and pulled them out realizing it was Lou Ellen who had been driving the car. They thanked him and got back home, thankful the car wasn't damaged and that Mr. Goodson probably wouldn't tell on them.

Annie had built a car port off the back of the house and then a large room with a bathroom. She ran a nursery school there for a short time. When she decided to shut the school down, Hugh pleaded with her to let him have it for his room and she gave in. This gave him and his friends a great deal of free-dom. Annie seldom came back there to check on them. They weren't old enough to drink yet, but they were able to get some cigarettes to smoke during their poker games.

Hugh, age 13, at Wadley house

One night, Hugh had the idea to set off a cherry bomb under the police car. The plan was to call the police to a house up the dirt road beside Hugh's house. They put a cherry bomb, with a long fuse on it, in the middle of the road and planned to light it when the police car came around the corner. It probably wouldn't work, but they were going to do it anyway.

Hugh called the police and told them there was a disturbance at the house up the road. They waited and sure enough, the police car came around the corner with old "Sputnik" driving; that's the nickname they gave the cop. They lit the fuse and ran into a vacant field to watch. Sputnik could see the fuse burning and stopped to see what it was. As he approached it, it went off. He jumped back, pulled his gun out, and started looking around shining his flashlight. The boys, Hugh, Tom Newton, and Don Goodson, were all scared they were going to get caught, but they made it back to Annie's house undetected.

Hugh just had to push things even further. He talked the

boys into going out to talk to the cop and ask what the noise was all about, because it had woken the baby! Don got a few scratches running through the field, and Tom couldn't sleep that night, but Hugh was pretty sure nothing would come of it and it didn't. They didn't get caught.

One summer, Hugh and Tom spent a couple of weeks at Old Town, Uncle Pressley's farm. There was a huge old house there, and Uncle Pressley never stayed there anymore. The boys had a tractor to ride around on and no one to bother them. They were too young to have a driver's license, but on the farm, on a tractor, it didn't matter.

However, they were old enough to be curious about girls and when Hugh found out about the Girl Scouts from Wadley coming to Magruder, the boys decided to sneak over and check it out. They planned to move some of the boards from the shack at the pool where the girls would change. If they moved the boards just a little, they could get a peek, and the girls wouldn't know. They even dug a trench big enough for the two of them to crawl into and camouflaged it with bushes. Hugh even found some binoculars for the event. Everything was going well until Tom had the binoculars and whispered, "Hey Hugh, there's your sister." Hugh got very upset and snatched the glasses away from Tom, and that was the end of that.

Later, the boys got a ride into Louisville. Hugh wanted to go to the library. Tom couldn't figure out what he was up to, because Hugh usually wasn't interested in books. Someone told him there was a book titled *For Boys Only* that showed detailed drawings of the female anatomy. The librarian caught them and told them to get out or she would tell their mothers. They thought that they wouldn't be known in Louisville, but the librarian knew their mothers by name, Annie and Eleanor. The boys never got in trouble, so she must not have told on them.

Grandmother Evans' house

Hugh and Don Goodson bought an old car for a few hundred dollars, maybe a Model T, and worked on it at Annie's. Did they ever get it running? I'm not really sure, but they had a lot of fun working on it.

One of the main places teenagers used to go to dance on Saturday night was McKinnies Pond. Annie would let Willa drive the car, and Hugh at fifteen and Ellen at fourteen would get to tag along—Hugh more often than Ellen. There wasn't a band but there was a jukebox, and jitterbug was the thing. You didn't have to have a date, just show up and have fun dancing; you could always find a partner. Hugh taught Ellen to do the jitterbug.

Grandmother Evans

When Grandmother got too old to drive, she gave her car to Annie. By then Hugh was fifteen and had his learner's license. It was about a 1950 green Dodge. Hugh would go by, pick up Grandmother in the old green car, and take her for a ride. It was fun for both of them; she got out of the house and he got to drive. The best part of this story is that it was Hugh's idea to do this. How many fifteen-year-olds volunteer to take their grandmother for a ride?

The old green car also went for some rough rides, when Hugh was sixteen and could take the car out by himself. The road that turns off Main Street to go by the grammar school was being repaired. They had put five or six mounds of dirt in a row along the road. Hugh came along and ran the car over the mounds. He went up and down the road several times fast, making the old car hop over the mounds. A small group of kids from the grammar school stopped to watch, as school had just let out. Having an audience just egged Hugh on. Charley Roy Hall was one of the kids in that small group of spectators.

Hugh shot a hole in the floor of Willa's bedroom. No one is sure exactly when this happened. It was easy to hide with a rug because it was right beside the bed. He must have been sitting on the side of the bed holding a rifle when it fired by accident.

Military school.

In the Fall of 1958, Hugh was sent off to Swanee Military Academy in Tennessee. It was his sophomore year of high school. He must have pulled one too many pranks. After a few months there, he ran away and made it to Atlanta. Sister Lea was in school at Emory University at the time. She had started using the first name Lea, which are her initials, instead of Lou Ellen when she went off to college. She gave him a ride from the north part of the city to south of the city. He called her when he got to Wadley and told her he had gotten a ride all the way from south Atlanta right to Annie's front door in Wadley.

All through high school, Hugh wore a red dinner jacket with black trim. He wore it all the time. No one seems to remember where he got it. In the ninth grade, he had worn a black leather jacket. He always had that bad boy image with long hair in a duck tail. Sometimes he would wear a pink shirt and turn the collar up like Elvis. Hugh was always very popular with all the girls. He was Mr. Wadley High when he was in the ninth grade according to the year book.

Hugh in 9th Grade.

One New Year's Eve, Hugh borrowed Lea's TR3 sports car to go to the dance in Louisville. Everyone was dressed up in semi-formal attire for the big dance. Lea had a date; that's why she let Hugh use her car. Ellen had a date with her friend, George, from Louisville. Hugh was by himself that night and seemed a little down about it. Everybody seemed to have a date but him. Ellen danced with him a few times, but he left before the dance was over.

On their way home, Ellen and her date noticed someone on the side of the road just before the bridges between Wadley and Louisville. It was Hugh. He had been in a wreck. The road was wet from the rain and there was a curve in the road right before the bridges. He had lost control and run the car off the road down the embankment toward the river. Ellen got out and made Hugh lie down beside the road. She put her new semiformal white sweater with a rabbit fur collar over him. Another car stopped and went to call an ambulance.

They only kept him for a little while in the emergency room because he was okay, except for a few small cuts and bruises. Unfortunately, the car was totaled.

Athens, Ga.
1/6/60

Dear Aunt Betsey,

Since you sent me your first letter of the year, I thought I would send you my first letter of the year.

I'm sorry about your dream, it must have been quite a shock when you heard about my accident. The accident an awful experience, but I think I learned a lesson from it. I don't think was the fault of the road as much as it was mine, I left the dance I was pretty lonely & disgusted after everybody had a date except me. I guess I was kind of feeling sorry for my self, and wasn't paying much attention to my driving the slick road.

I guess God must have really been riding in that other seat with me.

Tell Ellen that I'm awfully sorry about her dress, I guess she and everybody thought I was hurt pretty bad by the way I was acting, I tell you Aunt Betsy there haven't been many times in my life that I've been really scared, but this was

~~GEORGE WILKINS~~

one time I was scared to death.

I guess you have heard by now that the insurance co. is going to pay for Lou Ellen's car, I'm happy about that.

Don't forget to tell Ellen that I'm really grateful for her taking such good care of me.

Love,
Hugh

P. S.
Those Steaks sound mighty good.

Lea did get paid back by her insurance company so she could get another car. The family found out later that the sheriff of Jefferson County, who knew the Alexanders well, had removed the whiskey bottle from the car before the state patrol got there, so Hugh wouldn't get in more trouble.

In high school at Wadley, Hugh wasn't into playing sports much. He only played football his freshman year. The arts were more his style. He was in the high school band three years and captain of the band his senior year. He was in the drama club three years. All three years he was at Wadley High, he was in "Spring Frolics." His senior year he was in the senior play, "Duet for Two Hands." Hugh's band, "Alexander's Ragtime Band," played in Spring Frolics his senior year. He was also on the Literary Team and in the National Thespian Society his senior year.

He graduated from Wadley High School in 1960. At the graduation he gave a speech titled, "Education in the Changing Future." The motto of his class was "Whatever you do, do it well." In the Last Will and Testament of the yearbook his senior year Hugh wrote "I, Hugh Alexander, leave my everyday red and black dinner jacket to the next poor fool that thinks high school is one big party." He had worn such a jacket to school almost every day and it was sort of his trademark. Actually, Tom Newton had given him the idea for this testament and Hugh liked it so much he used it, because it fit him so well.

Graduation.

National Director
BLANDFORD JENNINGS
Clayton High School
Clayton, Mo.

Assistant National Director
DORIS M. MARSHALL
Helena High School
Helena, Mont.

Senior Councilor
BARBARA WELLINGTON
B. M. C. Durfee High School
Fall River, Mass.

Senior Councilor
JEAN E. DONAHEY
Senior High School
Brownsville, Pa.

The National Thespian Society

Devoted to the Advancement of Dramatic Arts in the Secondary Schools

LEON C. MILLER, Executive Secretary-Treasurer

COLLEGE HILL STATION   CINCINNATI 24, OHIO

To Whom It May Concern:

_____ *R. Lynn Woodall* _____, faculty

sponsor of Troupe ___ *2045* ___ of The National Thespian Society, and

___ *D. L. Hodge* ___, principal of the ___ *Wadley* ___

High School, *Wadley*, *Georgia*, recommend to you
            CITY   STATE

without any reservations Thespian ___ *Hugh Alexander* ___.

Membership in the National Thespian Society is awarded for meritorious participation in the dramatic arts program of the high school. In addition to meeting all rigid requirements of the national organization, a Thespian must discharge faithfully all local assignments and cooperate wholeheartedly in furthering all school activities with which he may be associated.

The bearer of this letter has passed all tests of participation, cooperation, loyalty, and honesty. The National Thespian Society thus considers it a privilege to call to your attention this student's interests and qualifications.

Very sincerely yours,

Leon C. Miller, Executive Sec'y-Treas.

THE NATIONAL THESPIAN SOCIETY

Publishers of

D R A M A T I C S

An Educational Magazine for Directors, Teachers, and Students of Dramatic Arts
Published October through May

CHAPTER FOUR

Life after Wadley

After high school, Hugh went to college at the University of Georgia. He started there the Fall of 1960 and dropped out, but I'm not sure exactly when. During his college years, he would drive back home to Wadley quite often and stop in Warrenton, Georgia, which was right on the way, between Athens and Wadley, to see Aunt Betsy. Sometimes he would have a friend with him, then Aunt Betsy would invite them to have supper with her and Uncle Howard. One of those times, Hugh had Hubert Jordon with him, and she didn't have much food. She opened a big can of Dinty Moore stew and some rice, and Hugh made her feel like they had a feast. Hugh loved Aunt Betsy, and one of the times he dropped by he brought her a pair of earrings. She loved him too, and the earrings remained special to her heart.

While Hugh was in Athens, he joined a sky diving club. They even parachuted a poor goat out of a plane. Hugh had a goat named "Damnit" when he was in college, I'm not sure if it was the same goat.

One weekend when Ellen was in Wadley, and Hugh was at home for the weekend, he told her he had something to show her. He had a pickup truck that he had rigged a parachute to the back of, and a long rope that reached to the cab. He wanted Ellen to pull the rope, which would in turn pull the parachute cord to open it. They took off down a dirt road, and Hugh got the pickup going fast. When he thought it was fast enough, he told Ellen to pull the rope. The parachute opened, and the truck went fishtailing all over the road, thankfully not in the ditch.

While Hugh was in Athens going to school, he and Ron Rachels lived together for a while in a place outside Athens near Winterville. It was an unpainted tenant house, on a turkey farm, within fifty feet of a building filled with white gobblers. They took the place because it was cheap and in the middle of nowhere, so they thought, we can have loud parties and no one will care. Also the wind usually blew in the opposite direction, so they didn't have to smell the turkeys much.

The birds were constantly being picked up by big trucks. The road into the farm was a graveled, asphalt-paved country road with ditches on both sides for drainage. To get the trucks in, drain pipes had been raised slightly higher than the road. The trucks pulled flatbed trailers much higher than the ones on large multi-axle trucks today. The entrance was also raised very high.

At the time, Hugh had a light blue MGA sports car. He always drove it with the top down, and he always wore his aviator sunglasses and had a scarf around his neck with the scarf flowing out behind him. You could see him coming from a distance and know it was him, quite a sight, like something out of

The blue MGA.

the movies. Hugh always had some sort of signature look.

One afternoon, Ron and the other roommate were getting out of their car, and they saw Hugh coming. Of course, it was the same scene, with the top down, the sunglasses, and the scarf blowing in the wind. He was driving fast, and they knew he would blow by the house, wave, continue down the road, then turn around, and come back, laughing like he always did.

This day was different because it was turkey pickup day. A truck with a turkey trailer had pulled in and was now backing slowly up to the slight grade and stopped just on top of the entrance, to look for cars. Hugh said that he thought the driver was waiting for him to pass and sped up. Suddenly, the driver gunned the engine to pass over the rise and was backing over the road into the field across the road. The front of the trailer wheels were on the slight rise. The rear wheels were actually entering the field raising the trailer. There were no wheels on the road, just the flatbed stretching across the road.

Hugh was speeding toward the flatbed and had no chance of stopping. His friends looked on at the scene unfolding, feeling helpless to do anything. Hugh went under the trailer!

He must have cleared it by inches. The truck engine was so loud at the time that his friends didn't know for sure what had happened. They thought that it might be rolling over the car. They couldn't see because they were on the driver's side of the truck.

They got down on their knees to look for the car and saw Hugh speeding down the road with his scarf flying behind him in the wind. Finally, after the truck cleared the road, they saw Hugh turn around about a quarter of a mile up the road and come flying back. He flew by them so fast that the car blew sand in their faces. He was just doing his victory lap. They could hear him laughing as he sped by.

When he got back to the house, they all tried to make light of what had just happened. In truth they were probably just trying to hide the fact that they were all so shaken up. That was Hugh—always the showman. It was just like him to turn a death-defying event into a light-hearted moment, as though he had done it on purpose.

As all the excitement settled down, Hugh asked us if we would not ever talk about what happened to anyone. We all agreed without questioning him. It was a great story, but we honored his wishes; we never mentioned it again.

In January 1963, Hugh went to an aviation school in Nevada to get trained to fly different types of planes. He already had a basic pilot license, but wanted to learn more so he could make a career out of flying. In Nevada, he learned to fly the old, double-winged Steermans, larger two engine and four engine planes, and old ex-bombers from World War II.

While he was in Nevada, Hugh wrote several letters to me. I've managed to hang onto one of them all these years.

He called me Pee Wee back them. I'm not sure how he came up with that nickname, but he was the only one that called me that.

After Nevada, he came back to Georgia to look for a job. He worked at Peachtree-Dekalb Airport for a while as a line worker, which meant he moved planes around when they needed to be moved for some reason.

On June 12, 1963, when Hugh received his inheritance from Uncle Pressley, he bought an Austin Healy car. It was white with red interior. He only kept it for a few months, but he had it all that summer. One of the times he came home to see us in Wadley, he took me for a ride in the Healy. We went out on

The white 1963 Austin Healy.

the road between Bartow and Wrightsville. We were going so fast that the speedometer on the round odometer went back to zero. We must have been going about 140 miles per hour. I'm guessing because the odometer only went up to 120. The top was down, and we were flying. Both of us were smiling. I wasn't afraid at all, because I completely trusted Hugh. For some reason, he didn't keep the Healy very long. He got rid of it and got a Ford van.

Letter from Hugh to Marianne from Nevada.

1/7/63
Minden, Nevada

Dear Pee Wee,

Thanks for the letter, I got it today.

I haven't had to much time to spend sight-seing but from what I've seen (most of it from the air) its really beauty. Almost identical to the scenery you see in cowboy movies. Nevada is two + ½ times larger than Ga. and only has a population of 300,000 which is about the same as that of Savannah so its really the wide-open spaces.

Have really been doing a lot of flying. Most of the time we fly the old double-wing planes called

Stearman's because they are still used a lot for crop-dusting we also fly the larger 2 engine planes similar to Easter's. Later on we will practice flying 4 engine planes old WW bombers- bought from the Air Force. Next week we are getting in a helicopter so I guess I'll go ahead and get to be a whirly-bird pilot too.

I have taken some pictures and as soon as they are developed I'll send them to Mother so you can see some of the planes we fly.

Love,
Hugh

P.S.
write again when you get a chance.

Hugh with the biplane he was trained to fly.

CHAPTER FIVE

Married Life and Working Career

In October, 1963, Hugh met his future wife, Delilah Baxter. They met at a party and were introduced by mutual friends. When they met, Hugh had the van and was working at the Peachtree Dekalb Airport. She was in school in Athens. He came back to Athens almost every weekend because all of his friends were there and he didn't know very many people in Atlanta.

Ellen, Hugh's cousin and favorite sidekick from childhood, was in college at Georgia Southern in Statesboro at this time.

Ellen at Georgia Southern.

One night out of the blue, Hugh showed up at her dorm. Since guys couldn't come up to the room, they sat in his van to talk. Hugh told her that he was tired of drinking his coffee by himself every morning, and that he had met Delilah. He said he was going to ask her to marry him, because she understood him and gave him such joy and peace. He said that if he wanted to stop along the side of the road to look at something, even something as simple as a flower, that she would sit there and look at it with him.

Wedding party.

She must have said yes, because they did get married on February 8, 1964. Hugh was living in Savannah at the time. The local TV station there found out that someone was getting married that afternoon in an airplane, so they came out to the airport. Hugh and Delilah were on the 6:00 p.m. news that evening. They were briefly interviewed before takeoff, and then flew over South Carolina to take their vows, with the pilot and minister on board. When they landed back in Savannah, their wedding party was waiting for them—John Maben, Jimmy Houser, Don Goodson, and Ellen, Delilah's roommate from school. They all went to a restaurant to celebrate and have lunch. Delilah remembers her first dance with her new husband; "Smoke Gets in Your Eyes" was playing on the juke box.

Delilah.

Hugh was taking some fight lessons in Savannah, and that was the first place they lived. They were only there for a few weeks when he got a job in Demopolis, Alabama. I was sixteen at the time, so Annie let me ride a bus by myself to visit them. Hugh had called and invited me. He also asked me to bring a few things and not tell Annie about it. I can't remember exactly what but it was something like a couple of plates, a pillowcase, a fork, and a spoon. This secret mission, I carried out successfully. I would sneak around the house and get the things to take to Demopolis when Annie was either asleep or out of the house and put them in my suitcase. She put me on the bus and never knew about my secret mission.

Delilah and Hugh married.

Delilah and Hugh.

After Alabama, they moved to Delray Beach, Florida. I remember going to Florida with Hugh and Don Goodson in Don's Triumph. There were only two seats, so I had to sit sideways behind the seats all the way to Delray Beach. I think we left Hugh down there, and I came back home with Don.

They stayed in Delray Beach a year or so, and their first child was born there. Julie, named after Julian Alexander, our father's brother, was born in December 1964.

Hugh went to Nicaragua every winter from 1965 to 1970. Delilah went down at least for a visit every year, except when she was pregnant with Causey in 1970. When I was a freshman in college, I went with Delilah to Nicaragua to visit Hugh on my Christmas break. It was the first time I had been out of the country.

That first morning at the hotel, Hugh told me how to say eggs and toast in Spanish, so I could go order breakfast. I think he just wanted to get me out of the room so they could be alone. I was so amazed when the waiter understood my Spanish and brought me my eggs and toast.

On that trip to Nicaragua, Hugh spent a whole afternoon with just me, which made me feel very special. We rode his motorcycle to the beach and stayed there a while, and then we went to a movie. The movie was in Spanish with English subtitles. I don't remember the name of the movie or even what it was about. I just remember being with my brother that I loved so much and feeling so very special that he would spend so much time with me.

I also have two letters from Hugh that he wrote to me from Nicaragua. By then he was calling me Marianne. He always signed them, Love, Hugh. As many times as I have moved in all these years, it's amazing that I've been able to hang onto them, but it's because Hugh was always so special to me. *(See pages 52-55)*

Hugh with Julie and Elizabeth.

In 1967, they moved to Louisville, Georgia, where Hugh worked for Jack Sliker out of a grass landing strip a few miles from Wadley off the highway between Wadley and Midville. They lived in a small house across from the Thermo King plant in Louisville first, then on Forest Avenue in Louisville, which is where they were living when Elizabeth was born on August 20, 1968. Jack's

Flying Service moved to a
modern airport in Louisville
about 1969. Together Hugh and
Jack flew Piper crop dusters
providing service for local
farmers. They also founded
Southern Aircraft, Inc., when
they moved to the Louisville
Airport. In August of 1969,
Hugh hired Byron Burt as their

Hugh striping his airplane in 1971 at the Louisville Airport.

maintenance man. It was Byron's job to keep all the planes
maintained and serviced.

When Alan Rachels was a young man, he worked for
Hugh for a short time at the Louisville Airport helping to
load the crop dusting planes. He remembers watching Hugh
spray crops one time, when he was flying low across the crops
to give good coverage. There was a power line at the edge of
the field and, as Hugh approached it to fly under it, the tail
of the plane snagged the line causing it to stretch out like a
slingshot and pull the plane upward. Momentarily, the plane
stopped in motion, then with a huge bang the line snapped
and the crop sprayer broke loose with a huge lunge forward
and Hugh flew away. Alan was standing not far away. It
happened so quickly, but Alan was wondering, "What in the
world was Hugh thinking?" Later, when Alan had a chance to
talk to Hugh, he commented in his usual confident demeanor,
"It was just another lucky day."

In about 1970, Hugh and Delilah bought Aunt Sally's
house in Louisville. They were living there when I was at the
University of Georgia. That summer, I was in school and Annie

The house Hugh bought from Aunt Sally.

had gone to Europe. I dropped out of school early in the quarter, though I can't remember why now. I guess I got sick and missed too many classes to make up. Anyway, I couldn't stay in Wadley by myself, so I asked Hugh if I could stay with them till Annie got home. He said yes, of course.

Uncle Pressley had loaned me the money to get a car with the agreement that I would pay him back when I received my inheritance at twenty-one-years-old from Aunt Minnie and Uncle Billy. Having my own car was great. I had turned twenty-one in January, and had paid Uncle Pressley back in full.

While staying with Hugh and Delilah that summer, one night I came home at eleven, just as was supposed to. I asked

Aunt Sally and Marianne.

Hugh if I could go back out because there was a friend that needed a ride home. Hugh could have just said no, but instead he said, "I don't think that's a good idea, but you're an adult and you can make up your own mind."

Well, I would never do anything that Hugh didn't want me to do, so of course, I didn't go. I idolized him, so I didn't ever want him to

Delilah, Julie, and Hugh.

be disappointed in me. Hugh knew just how to handle the situation. He was very mature and wise for someone only twenty-seven- years-old. He would have been a great father for his teenage kids.

Flying with Hugh was always exciting, and I was never afraid. I trusted him completely. He would sometimes do stunts like loops and spins. It was fun and exhilarating, never scary. I never got to go to an air race, however.

After Hugh moved back near home, he would often buzz Annie's house in Wadley by flying low and waving the wing of his plane. We would all go out in the yard to wave back at him. He even saw Aunt Betsy one time going back to Warrenton after visiting Grandmother, and recognized her car. He waved his wing to get her attention, flew low and yelled, "Hi Aunt Betsy." She knew right away it was Hugh. Who else could it be?

Betsy and Annie.

Another time, Aunt Betsy happened to be passing by, and there was Hugh in a field with his plane on the ground. She stopped to see what was wrong. He was having some kind of problem and asked Aunt Betsy if she had a coat hanger in her car. She yes that she did happen to have one, and Hugh used it to somehow fix whatever was wrong until he could get back to the airport and let the mechanic look at it.

It was obvious that Hugh loved his family. He used to drive his Grandmother around when he was a teenager and when he would come back home as an adult, in the last few years of her life, he would still go by and take her for a ride. By then she was very small and frail. Hugh would pick her up in his arms like a child, put her in the car, and say, "Come on little doll; let's go for a ride." She didn't get out much, and this was a great treat for her.

Hugh loved his children, and this was also obvious. Lea can remember seeing him under the kitchen table with Julie pretending they were flying an airplane. I can remember Hugh rolling in the grass with his kids in the front yard and Delilah laughing and saying, "What will the neighbors think?"

Delilah never knew who would be in the kitchen when she woke up and Hugh wasn't in bed. He had insomnia and might be at the kitchen table talking to Lord knows who in the middle of the night. Sometimes he would go to the Huddle House when he couldn't sleep. You can run into some weird folks late at night at the Huddle House.

After moving back to Louisville, Hugh had to find a dentist. He didn't like

Julie and Hugh.

getting the shots that most dentists use. He found a dentist that was a friend of a relative, that used gas. Hugh made an appointment, and when he arrived he told the dentist that he had been "flying under the radar." At the time the dentist thought Hugh had meant he had been driving fast. Later, he found out what Hugh meant was that he had flown to Macon and not programmed and filed his flight

Hugh and Julie.

plan as you are supposed to do because he was in a hurry. He literally flew under the radar so he wouldn't get caught breaking the rules.

Delilah, Hugh, Elizabeth, and Julie.

The two letters that Hugh wrote to Marianne from Nicaragua.

October 29, 1966
Sunday Afternoon
León, Nicaragua

Dear Marianne,

Appreciated the letter, My God, 5 pages I will never live up to that.

My work has slowed down considerably I usually work one day and off two for one week and then work two and have one off the next week. Actually I had just soon not have the days off because there is nothing to do. The reason the work slowed down so much is because my boss man has 2 planes the other one is a Call Air (a small plane similar to Jack's pawnees) It was in the shop for 3 weeks having a engine overhaul and I had to spray all the cotton by myself. They offered to lease another plane to help me, but I told they must not have ever seen a Georgia boy drive an airplane and not to lease another ship until I got behind. I managed to keep up and with this last week put out 100,000 gals in my first month. We get paid by the gals. of insecticide we spray and 100,000 gals. figures out to $6,500. Thats more than I made in 6 months at home, so if things hold out for the next three months old Hugh Baby is going to be driving one of them Jaguars around just as soon as I get back.

— 2 —

None of the Gringos own airplanes down here, we all work just as pilots consequently ~~so~~ its like a race to see who can do the "mostest" in the "leastest" anyway I really gave them a record to break. One day about 2 weeks ago I put out 8,000 galns in one day and in 8 hours flight time, the previous record was 5,700 gals. so I have been ~~xxxx~~ somewhat of a celebrity here lately. Its not all fun and games though, five of the fellows working with us last year were killed in the states this past summer and two of the guys ~~xx~~ have been killed here this year already. Damn its been a bad year on pilots, if I could keep this job for 3 or 4 more years I think Ill hang up my hard hat and retire. Well guess Ill get off the sentimental tangent. Have you asked Annie about you coming down yet? You know we will have to have her permission.

You asked about the Ocelots down here. They look just like Jaguars, in fact a lot of stupid turists buy them thinking they are Jaguars. The only difference is that they don't get as big. They cost about $20.00
Got to run
Love
Hugh

P. S. you had better hurry up and decide what day you are coming down and get Delilah to make airline reservations for you by November 10th at the latest. You know if they are booked up there is no other way to get down here.

14 October
León, Nicaragua
C.A.

Dear Marianne,

Thanks for th letter, sorry it has taken me so long to reply, but thanks to th little man upstairs, have been busy as hell lately. I have been real lucky so far, got a damn good seat my first day down here — am driving a new Snow S2C with a 600 H.P. Pratt & Whitney engine up front. I realize you probably don't know what that is, but you can do some research and find out, or I'll send you a picture if they ever come back. It takes about a month to get them developed down here.

Have you taken any flying lessons yet? You know I was thinking if you could just get your student permit and solo (it only takes 8-10 hours instruction) sometimes this fall or winter you could use my plane to get the other 30 hours in this spring It takes 40 hours for a private License, this would be a hell of a lot cheaper than renting one for the entire 40 hours. If you do take any lessons though be sure you start in a plane with a tailwheel rather than a a nosewheel, because you wouldn't be able to fly mine unless you do. It might be hard to locate one with a tailwheel, but I'm pretty sure there is a instructor with one in Jefferson, Ga which is close to Gainsville or the instructor in Gainsville might have one. Delilah knows where the airport is in Jefferson she has been there with me before. Any of the following A/c would be suitable: Cessna 140, J-3 cub or PA-11 or PA-12 or PA-18, or an Aronca or Luscombe.

You said you met a couple of huns from Port St. Joe, we were down there some this summer one of our mosquito contracts was near there in Chattahochee, Fla.

Delilah is supposed to come down about December 17th. I know annie probably wouldn't let you come before xmas, but if you still want to maybe you could come on the 27th or so down Here then you could still spend at least a week before having to get back to school.

Write again soon & let me know whats going on and your plans about coming down.

Love
Hugh

Stewball

Oh Stewball was a racehorse, and I wish he were mine.
He never drank water, he always drank wine.

His bridle was silver, his mane it was gold.
And the worth of his saddle has never been told.

Oh the fairgrounds were crowded, and Stewball was there
But the betting was heavy on the bay and the mare.

And a-way up yonder, ahead of them all,
Came a-prancin' and a-dancin' my noble Stewball.

I bet on the grey mare, I bet on the bay
If I'd have bet on ol' Stewball, I'd be a free man today.

Oh the hoot owl, she hollers, and the turtle dove moans.
I'm a poor boy in trouble, I'm a long way from home.

Oh Stewball was a racehorse, and I wish he were mine.
He never drank water, he always drank wine.

CHAPTER SIX

Hugh's Racing Career

Hugh's air racing career began in 1970 when he bought his World War II, AT6, fighter plane, and named it "Stewball." This type of plane was typically used in air racing.

Stewball was the name of a race horse foaled in England in 1741. He won many races there and was then sent to Ireland, where he won six races in 1752, being the top-earning runner of that year in Ireland. The most famous race was on the Plains of Kildare, Ireland, and is the subject of the lyrics of the song, "Stewball."

HUGH ALEXANDER

Hugh's plane, Stewball.

The AT6, commonly called the T6, was the most widely used training airplane in history, nicknamed, the "Texan." This plane started being used in air races in the late 1960's and early 1970's. In the air races, it had to be raced strictly stock production without modifying the engine. Of course, all the military equipment was taken out, and the paint jobs were changed.

The engine was a Pratt and Whitney R-1340 radial engine, 450 hp. Races are guaranteed to be competitive and racing times very close when the planes are required to be left in stock condition. Races can be won and lost by as close as 1/5 second or 0.76 mph!

On April 16-19, in Ft. Lauderdale, Florida, an air race was held by the Atlantic Coast Air Races Organization. There were three classes in the race. The course was a 3.189-mile oval course. In the AT6 class there were twenty that qualified. Hugh placed third with a speed of 192.62 mph. This was amazing because it was his first race. John Mosby came in first at 195.24 mph and Richard Minges came in second at 193.60

mph. These were the trials to qualify for the race.

Hugh Alexander
Louisville, Georgia

On the day of the race, it was won by Ben Hall at 198.25 mph, which broke a record that had been set at Reno in 1969. Minges came in second at 190.22 mph and John Trainor third at 188.59 mph.

The other two classes for the race were the sport biplane and the Formula One class. The sport biplane class

Stewball

speed was between 157 to 173 mph. The Formula One class was the fastest, between 210 to 230 mph.

Hugh's second air race was in 1971 at Wilson, North Carolina, on May 15-16, at the Old Wilson Airport. For this race there were only two classes, the AT6 and the Formula One. The course was 3.00 miles, they are always oval. Hugh and Stewball qualified at 192.86 mph for the AT6 race. The race was won by Richard Minges at 198.0 mph with Hugh coming in second at 196.5 mph, and this was only his second race. Minges was also in the second race with his Formula One and came in second at 212.49 mph. Hugh and Richard Minges

Formula One plane flown by Hugh.

became good friends both on and off the air racing field.

The Third Annual Wilson Air Race was held on May 20-21, 1972. The AT6 class only drew six pilots. Hugh came in first in the qualifying trials at 204.82 mph. the course was 2.424 miles for eight laps. Hugh won the race at 200.00 mph. This was only his third race.

Transpo 72 was held from May 27 to June 4 at Dulles International Airport near Washington D.C. and was intended to be one of the greatest air shows in history, comparable to the Paris Air Show. All hope was lost after the first one because of big financial losses, traffic problems, and several fatal accidents during the show.

The Formula One race was on the last day, June 4 and was the only competitive event. There were eleven entries. Hugh was flying a Formula One in the race, owned by a Santa Ana, California man. In the qualifying run on June 3, as three planes rounded the first turn of the 3.03 mile course, a midair collision occurred when Hugh's plane slid upward from the centrifugal force of the turn and hit another plane. The other pilot, Charles

Andrews, was not hurt. He managed to land his damaged plane safely. Unfortunately, Hugh was killed instantly.

Family left behind included his wife, Delilah, two daughters, Julie, age seven and Elizabeth, age three, and one son, Hugh Causey Alexander, III, one-year-old.

Causey, Julie, Liz, and Delilah

Stewball now.

The late Hugh Alexander of Louisville, Georgia, leaps out of the cockpit of his #30, "Stewball," after winning the T-6 Championship Race at Wilson, N.C., in 1972. Hugh lost his life a very short time later while competing in a Formula I Race at Transpo '72 in Chantilly, Virginia. (John Tegler photo)

The late Ed Snyder of Atlantic Beach, Florida, stands on the wing of his #99, "Mongoose," at Alton, Illinois in 1970. Ed was the T-6 Championship winner at Wilson, North Carolina in 1970 and was a contender in a great many other races. He, too, tragically lost his life in one of the two T-6 accidents in the same race at New Jersey in 1971. (John Tegler photo)

T-6D, now re-numbered #33 and called the "Fayetteville Special." This T-6 Championship Race was one which people will talk about for years. Nine aircraft, eight entrants plus the pace plane, roared across the starting line in what looked like a scene from "Tora, Tora, Tora." They were going for the "Sky Prints Trophy," and, to make things more interesting in addition to the eight entries, the aircraft were set up in a reverse starting order with the fastest qualifier in the tail-end position rather than in the pole position as would be normal. Needless to say, the race was furious with at least twenty-four passes being made and, at the end, it was Minges who crossed the finish line first with a speed of 198 mph flat! Hugh Alexander was right behind in second with Ed Snyder again in third.

The remainder of the 1971 season belonged to Bob Mitchem and he became the first T-6 competitor to win two Championship Events in one year. The first of these races was the New Jersey Nationals which were, unfortunately, the scene of two separate T-6 accidents in a single heat race in which four very fine pilots and competitors were lost; Richard Minges, Ed Snyder, Vic Baker and Jay Quinn. This constituted the largest single loss of life and the worst accident in the his-

tory of the sport. Even though the participants were stunned and grieved by these accidents, the races were continued and, on Sunday, Bob Mitchem moved the beautiful red and white "Miss Colorado" smoothly around the course to win the Championship at 199.16 mph with Hugh Alexander who had led the race in the early laps in second. It had been an excellent race considering the mood that all of these pilots were in due to the previous day's occurrences, and it showed the professionalism of all.

At Reno in 1971, Bob Mitchem pulled off his fourth Championship Victory in T-6 Competition in a race in which, at least for him, there was very little competition. He led on the Race Horse Start. He led around the Scatter Pylon. He led into the first lap and extended his lead on every lap thereafter to win going away with a speed that was 10 mph faster than the second place airplane. In so doing, he set a new competitive Heat Record for the Class of 205.85 mph. The second place finisher has since become the only other man to win four T-6 Championship Races. Pat Palmer had not even been scheduled to be in this Championship Race. He had already competed in the Silver or Consolation Race and was the stand-by for the Championship. He started in this race

when it was discovered that one of the scheduled participants, Don Phillippi, did not have operating radio equipment.

Hugh Alexander, who had been a challenger for some time, became the seventh man to win a T-6 Championship Event. In his black and red T-6B, #30, "Stewball," he notched his T-6 Championship Win at the first race of the 1972 season at Wilson, North Carolina. Alexander had won at 200 mph even, but had had to fight off the determined efforts of rookie, "Mac" McClain, who finished in the second position in that race and then went on to claim the rest of the 1972 season, which was his first year of active competition in the sport, as his own. Hugh Alexander would undoubtedly have been a winner several more times in T-6 Racing and would have more than likely been involved in some outstanding duels with Mac McClain and others but, sadly, he, too, was lost while competing in a Formula I Race at Transpo '72.

In his orange and checkerboard #25 T-6C, "Miss Eufaula," Roy "Mac" McClain quickly became the eighth competitor to win a T-6 Championship Race, and, just as quickly, became only the second man to win two of these Championships in one season. Mac dominated the Class at the Texas

Article from *Sport Flying*.

CHAPTER SEVEN

The Gift

The gift I was given through the tragedy of losing my brother was the single most important event of my life. I was only twenty-four-years-old, and he was twenty-nine. Although much of our communication was nonverbal, there was a deep connection between us. We could be in a room full of people and know exactly what each other was thinking about the conversation or the situation around us.

As a young kid, I idolized Hugh. He was my hero. He was my cool older brother. He turned me on to the music of the early sixties—folk music like Bob Dylan and Joan Baez, jazz like Mose Allison, and rock n' roll like Bo Diddley.

In June of 1972, he was going to Transpo 72 being held near Washington, D.C. Since I had spent the night with them the night before, I took Hugh to the Louisville airport the morning he left to go to the race, and then I drove back to Athens, Georgia, where I was living at the time.

The next morning, the phone call came. It was my sister, Lea. There had been a fatal accident. Another plane had clipped the wing of Hugh's plane in the air race, and he had been killed instantly.

At first there was a feeling of disbelief. I was in shock. Unable to drive myself, a friend drove me to my brother's house, in Louisville, Georgia. I stayed with his wife, Delilah, and his three children for about a week.

They had only been married for eight years, and I had become close to Delilah. In some ways she felt more like a sister than a sister-in-law. She was easy to talk to, and it felt only natural to stay with her and the children during this very stressful time. The children were so young; Julie was seven, Elizabeth four, and Causey was a one-year-old.

The only other person in the house with us was Tony. She was the wife of a pilot friend of Hugh and Delilah's. Her husband had been killed a year earlier in a plane crash. At some point, Tony and I were sent on an errand. I can't remember if we went to the grocery store or what, but it was long enough to have a significant conversation.

We discovered that we both were interested in meditation, health, and exercise. She reminded me that during times of stress, meditation and yoga could be very helpful. She had asked, how I was doing, and I had to admit, I hadn't slept much and eaten much since I heard about Hugh. When we got back to the house, I decided to try and rest. I found an empty bedroom and lay down. I closed my eyes and tried to meditate.

Then something unusual happened. I became aware of my heartbeat, without physically monitoring my pulse. I also became aware of my breathing. I noticed that I seemed to be able to control my heartbeat, mentally.

There is a prayer called the Jesus Prayer that I remembered from a book written by an anonymous Russian monk, *The Way of a Pilgrim*. The prayer goes like this, "Lord Jesus Christ, have mercy on me." I began to repeat the prayer like a mantra.

In the book, the monk worked for months trying to coordinate his breath and heartbeat with the prayer. I decided to see if I could do it. My breath fell right into the rhythm of the prayer, and I was still aware of my heartbeat without touching my pulse. I kept repeating the prayer, and I was able to set my heartbeat into the rhythm also. So it went like this, on the first phrase, "Lord Jesus Christ," two heartbeats and a breath in, and on the second phrase, "have mercy on me," two heartbeats and a breath out." Amazing, I was doing it! I couldn't believe it. Was I really controlling my heartbeat? Was I really doing something it took the monk months to master?

We're not supposed to be able to do that, so I decided to see if I was really controlling my heartbeat. I stopped repeating the prayer and lay still with my eyes closed. I mentally tried to speed up and then slow down my heartbeat and to my amazement, I was able to do it. I was still aware of my heartbeat without touching my pulse, and I played with this mentally for a short time. I was controlling my heartbeat!

This was a profound experience for me, because I realized, this was a mind over matter experience. If it was true in one instance, it was true in other instances. For me, this was proof that mind over matter experiences are possible. They can and do happen.

Even at twenty-four-years-old I had read many books on religion, philosophy, metaphysics, and mysticism. Before, I had intellectualized about these subjects and thought they were very interesting. The experience of controlling my heartbeat, had given me proof.

This experience was a turning point for me. Instead of feeling weak and confused about my brother's death, I began to feel strong and clear headed. My thoughts began to race. My intellect was stimulated. I felt a heightened sense of awareness. Insights simply came to me, and I felt blissful and connected to everything in the Universe. I never felt so much Joy, such a feeling of well-being. Was this a glimpse of Nirvana? Was I experiencing the higher consciousness I had read about? Was this what Maslow meant by what a peak experience was? Was this the kind of spiritual experience that Emerson wrote about? The things my intellect had not been able to understand were now perfectly clear. I was connected to my higher self.

This experience of heightened awareness lasted most intensely for about a week and then tapered off over a period of several weeks. During this time, I confided in a few people close to me and tried to describe what I was going through. The only words that I could find to say was that I felt like I had been spiritually reborn. I didn't hear a voice, or see a vision, but I could feel the presence of my higher power as surely as if it were standing in front of me. The insights that came were just suddenly in my thoughts, which is different from hearing a voice. I believe this is what is known as intuitive knowing. This is what Helena Blavatsky meant by "the voice of silence." This is how our higher consciousness talks to us when we are connected and the pipe way is open to the Divine that is within all of us.

On a day trip to Wadley to see the rest of the family, I got a chance to talk to Uncle Bubba, my mother's brother. I explained what I was going through, and he seemed to understand exactly what I was talking about. He said that he had had a spiritual experience himself, a long time ago, that had a profound effect on him. It was very reassuring to me, to know that he understood. The love and reassurance he showed me gave me so much strength and helped me when I needed it the most.

Because this experience was so intense and lasted for such a long time, I was afraid at one point, that I would never be normal again. Even though the experience was blissful, it was physically taxing. I wasn't sleeping or eating much, and I was worried that I might have a nervous breakdown. Thank goodness Tony, my brother's friend, was there, and she was able to reassure me that I would get back to normal. The intensity did begin to diminish and become more manageable. After I went back to Athens, it was several weeks before I was back to "normal."

What I experienced when Hugh died happened a very long time ago, but it was the single most important event of my life and it changed me forever. I believe that I experienced God or my higher power, directly, God being the Divine spark that we all have within us. All humans possess the ability to connect to the Divine in this way. I talk to God through prayer, affirmations, and visualization, and God talks to me through dreams, intuition, and synchronicities. I know that God exists and that my life is being guided by the Divine.

This gift that has given me an undeniable belief in the Divine is a gift that can never be repaid. It was given to me through the loss of my brother, who I was very close to, and loved dearly. This book is a small gift to his memory and to his children, so that they can know what a wonderful person he was. My hope is that this book will be kept in the family for many generations, so that Hugh's grandchildren and great, great grandchildren can know him. He was truly a very special human being.

Chapter Eight

After Hugh Had Left Us

The funeral was held in Vidette, Georgia, a few days later at the Presbyterian Church. There was also a graveside service. Hugh was placed near his father on the family plot at the Vidette Cemetery.

Planes flew over in a ceremonial formation with one going off on its own, symbolizing the loss of a fellow pilot. That evening all of us went over to Jack and Madelyn's house. Everyone needed to unwind a little. I'm sure Hugh was there with us in spirit.

One of Hugh's lifelong sidekicks remembers the last time she talked to him. It was Ellen, his cousin. She said he had called right before he had left to go to that air race in D.C. and they had made plans to get together so her husband, George, could get to know him and Delilah. He also wanted her to come to an air show in Louisville, Georgia, he was doing to raise money for the Boy Scouts. The morning of the show Ellen's son, Kurt, woke up with a fever of 103 degrees, so she wasn't able to go.

At the time she didn't know that she would never see Hugh again. That last time she had talked to him on the phone, she had later found out that she had hurt his feelings unintentionally. She had told him that she would come to the air show in Louisville if she didn't have anything better to do. Of course, she was just kidding, but being sensitive, Hugh had his feelings hurt. After all, Ellen was his childhood sidekick that had always been there for him.

Ellen anguished over this for months after the loss of Hugh and felt terrible knowing that she had hurt his feelings in their last conversation. Then one night she had a dream. She had had many dreams about Hugh, but this one was so real. Hugh was out in space with a fire proof suit on. He said he wanted to let her know that he was okay. He said the fire didn't hurt him in the plane crash and not to worry, that he knew she was kidding about the air show. He had come to visit her and let her know he was all right.

Years later, Ellen had another "visit" from Hugh in the form of a dream. It was right before the Evans Family reunion at the Dillard House. He said he just wanted to check in with her to let her know he was still okay and to tell the family hello.

Then he said he had to go back. Just like the other dream, it was very real. At the reunion, Ellen told Delilah about the dream. She asked her when did she have the dream and Ellen told her it was on Hugh's birthday. Ellen hadn't remembered the dream was on his birthday till later.

There were so many people that loved Hugh, and that still do. He is remembered as someone who was always happy, confident, charismatic, flamboyant, carefree, and fearless, who loved his family. He could be mischievous but he was also very caring. When you met him, he was the kind of person you didn't forget.

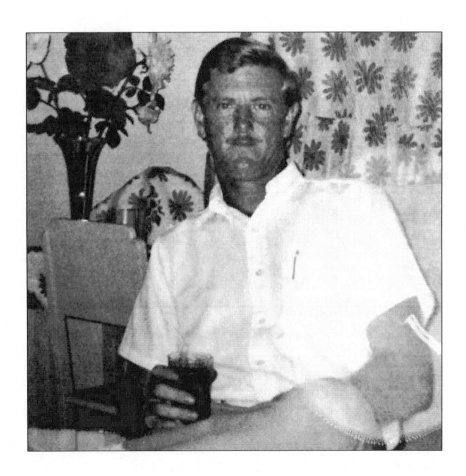

us and Farmer
ADLEY HERALD

IA, THURSDAY, MAY 3, 1973   LEGAL ORGAN OF JEFFERSON COUNTY   10c Per Copy

CUTTING THE RIBBON THE HARD WAY ! Ribbons are usually cut with a pair of scissors. Jim Holland from Pompano Beach, Florida does it the hard way. A red ribbon is strung between two 18 feet high metal poles that are only slightly further apart than the wingspan of Jim's little bi-plane. He then flys upside down, yet, just above the surface of the runway and shatters the ribbon to bit with his propellar. Holland is one of the star performers at the big aerial extravaganza scheduled next Sunday at the Louisville Airport.

Wadley Names
Projects For

Big Air Show To Be
Staged Here Sunday

CUTTING THE RIBBON THE HARD WAY ! Ribbons are usually cut with a pair of scissors. Jim Holland from Pompano Beach, Florida does it the hard way. A red ribbon is strung between two 18 feet high metal poles that are only slightly further apart than the wingspan of Jim's little bi-plane. He then flys upside down, yet, just above the surface of the runway and shatters the ribbon to bit with his propellar. Holland is one of the star performers at the big aerial extravaganza scheduled next Sunday at the Louisville Airport.

Wadley Names Projects For Revenue Funds

Wadley City Manager, Charles Warnock, announced this week that the Wadley Mayor and Council had given approval to two projects which will utilize the estimated $16,670.00 in Revenue Sharing Funds due the city.

According to Mr. Warnock, $13,492.00 will be used for the construction of a water main to supply the new plant of McLaurin Corp., a Division of Kayser-Roth Hosiery Co., Inc., of Burlington, N. C., which will be located on the U. S. 1 by-pass adjacent to Battle Lumber Company.

This line will also serve to increase the water capacity at Battle Lumber Company.

Some $3,178.00 of the funds will be used to purchase a new Police Patrol Car, Mr. Warnock said.

Big Air Show To Be Staged Here Sunday

Members of the Louisville Explorer Scout Post 252 will present their second annual Air Show at the Louisville Municipal Airport Sunday afternoon, May 6, beginning at 2:30 p.m. This year's show will be performed by the Jim Holland Air Shows, Inc.

Some 2,000 persons witnessed last year's spectacular show and the Scouts are hoping that this year's event will draw in the neighborhood of 5,000.

Advance tickets are being sold which will entitle the holder to a seat in the bleachers. Tickets can also be purchased at the gate.

Concession stands will be in operation under the supervision of the Scouts and their leaders.

This year's show has been dedicated to the memory of the late Hugh C. Alexander, a local pilot who was killed in an air race last spring.

Jim Holland and his team are nationally known for their precision aerobatic maneuvers and are expected to add thrill after thrill for the spectactors.

COME TO THE NATIONAL AIR RACES

JUNE 2, 3, 4, 5, 6
Wed.   Thur.   Fri.   Sat.   Sun.

RAIN DATE JUNE 7th.

CAPE MAY COUNTY, N.J. AIRPORT

WORLDS FASTEST MOTOR SPORT

FIRST TIME ON THE EAST COAST

★ **THE UNLIMITED CLASS** W.W. II FIGHTER PLANES P-51 — BEARCATS

RACING AT SPEEDS UP TO 450 MPH
50 FEET OFF THE GROUND!

★ **4 MAIN RACING EVENTS**
AT-6 FORMULA 1 BI-PLANES UNLIMITED

★ **MILITARY PRECISION TEAM**
★ **COMPLETE AIR SHOW**
INCLUDING AEROBATICS & PARACHUTING

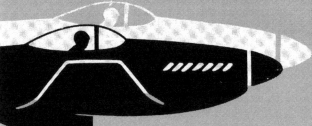

WRITE FOR TICKETS

SEASON (ALL 3 Days)
ADULT $15.00
CHILD $7.00

DAILY GRANDSTAND
(June 4, 5, & 6)
ADULT $6.00
CHILD $3.00

DAILY GENERAL ADMISSION
(June 4,5 & 6)
ADULT $5.00
CHILD $2.00

QUALIFYING DAYS (June 2 & 3)
FREE ADMISSION
FREE PARKING
NATIONAL AIR RACES
Cape May County, N.J. Airport
Box 746, Wildwood, N.J. 08260
(609) 886-2035

GENERAL INFORMATION

The National Air Races are held annually at Cape May County Airport, located 38 miles south of Atlantic City, New Jersey, on the Garden State Parkway. The airfield is 8 miles southwest of Sea Isle Omni (Washington Sectional).

Bus service is available from resort hotel and motel areas. Woodbine and Ocean i City airports. Allegheny Commuter service from Philadelphia.

QUALIFYING DAYS for all classes—June 2 and 3 from 10 a.m. to 6 p.m. FREE ADMISSION.

RACING and full support air show—June 4, 5 & 6 starting 12 noon. Five hours racing and Air Show.

CLOSED—COURSE PYLON RACING—each day in each of the four classes. UNLIMITED, Formula I, Sport Bi-Plane, AT6/SNJ.

CAPE MAY COUNTY AIRPORT will be closed to all incoming air traffic on qualifying and racing days from 11 a.m. to 6 p.m.

TEMPORARY FAA TOWER will be located on field. Frequencies, control and traffic information will be published in the Airman Information Manual.

15,000 GRANDSTAND SEATS will be available.

These Air Races are sanctioned by NAA and the PRPA.

PRINTED IN U.S.A.

ADDENDUM

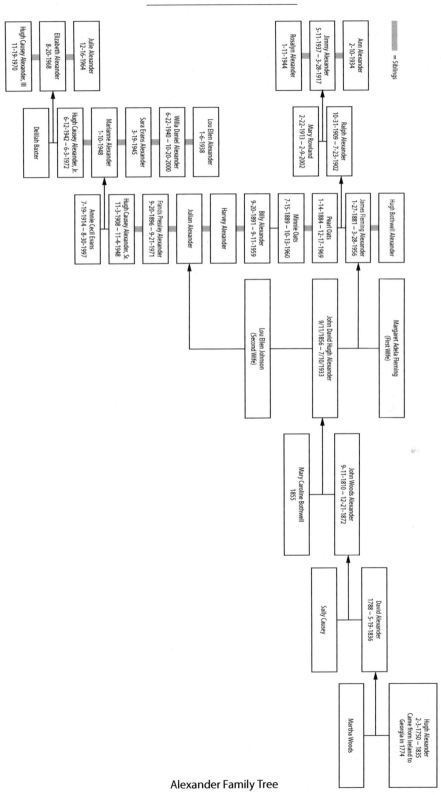

= Siblings

Hugh Causey Alexander, III
11-19-1970

Elizabeth Alexander
8-20-1968

Julie Alexander
12-16-1964

Delilah Baxter

Hugh Causey Alexander, Jr.
6-12-1942 – 6-3-1972

Marianne Alexander
1-10-1948

Sara Evans Alexander
3-19-1945

Willa Daniel Alexander
6-22-1940 – 10-20-2000

Lou Ellen Alexander
1-6-1938

Annie Cecil Evans
7-19-1914 – 8-30-1997

Hugh Causey Alexander, Sr.
11-3-1908 – 11-4-1948

Francis Presley Alexander
9-20-1896 – 9-21-1971

Julian Alexander

Harvey Alexander

Billy Alexander
9-20-1891 – 9-11-1959

Minnie Oats
7-15-1899 – 10-13-1960

Pearl Oats
1-14-1884 – 12-17-1969

James Fleming Alexander
1-27-1881 – 3-28-1956

Hugh Bothwell Alexander

Rosalyn Alexander
1-11-1944

Jimmy Alexander
5-11-1937 – 3-28-1917

Ann Alexander
2-10-1934

Mary Rowland
2-22-1913 – 2-9-2002

Ralph Alexander
10-31-1909 – 7-23-1902

Lou Ellen Johnson
(Second Wife)

John David Hugh Alexander
9/11/1856 – 7/10/1933

Margaret Adela Fleming
(First Wife)

Mary Caroline Bothwell
1855

John Woods Alexander
9-11-1810 – 12-21-1872

Sally Causey

David Alexander
1788 – 5-19-1836

Martha Woods

Hugh Alexander
2-3-1750 – 1835
Came from Ireland to
Georgia in 1774

Alexander Family Tree

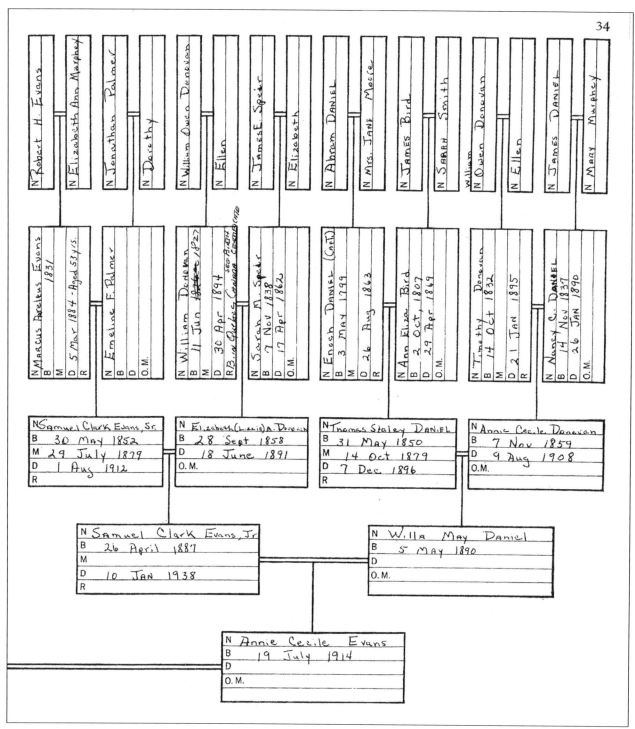

The Evans Family Tree.

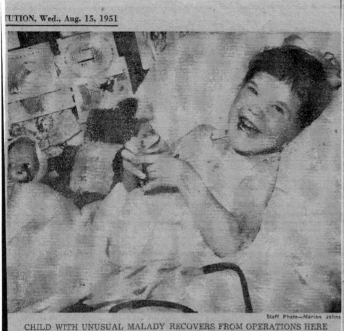

TUTION, Wed., Aug. 15, 1951

Staff Photo—Marion Johns

CHILD WITH UNUSUAL MALADY RECOVERS FROM OPERATIONS HERE
Marianne Alexander, of Louisville, is Nurses' "Pet" at St. Joseph's Infirmary

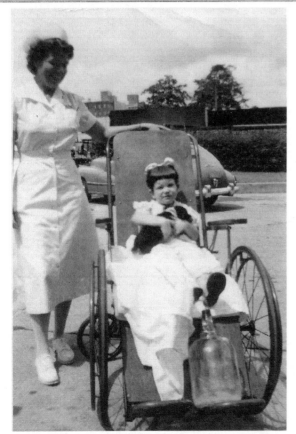

Marianne and her puppy, Mac, given to her by Doctor McDonald.

LOTS OF FIGHT IN HER

Marianne, 3, Survives 5 Serious Operations

By KATHERINE BARNWELL

Winsome three-year-old Marianne Alexander has "a lot of fight" in her.

Her mother, Mrs. H. C. Alexander, says that's why Marianne has survived five serious operations.

The dark-eyed little girl, a patient at St. Joseph's Infirmary, recently underwent operations on both her kidneys.

A staff physician said the case was rare. He estimated not one child in a million has had two such operations.

The doctor said Marianne's malady was similar to that of Forrest "Nubbins" Hoffman, the little Colorado boy who became famous by celebrating Christmas early. "Nubbins" later died.

Marianne's doctor said her case was unusual in that both her kidneys were affected. And he believes Marianne is "going to be all right."

Born with several "obstructions" of the kidneys, tubes and bladder, Marianne was a pale, sickly baby. Doctors told her mother they doubted she would live six months.

SURGERY AT SIX MONTHS

She first underwent surgery when she was six months old—and she has been in and out of hospitals ever since.

Her current hospital stint already has stretched to seven weeks. The surgeon removed part of her right kidney pelvis and enlarged the opening to the ureter (tube leading to the bladder) four weeks ago.

He performed the same operation on the left kidney two weeks ago.

Mrs. Alexander, who lives in Louisville, Ga., said Marianne would be here at least two more weeks. But Marianne doesn't mind much. She knows all the nurses, sisters, many of the patients, the elevator operator and even the cook at the hospital— and they shower her with attention.

64 GET-WELL CARDS

Marianne has received 64 get-well cards and she knows who sent each one.

The hospital cook brought her two bouquets of flowers. Her doctor gave her a puppy which she kept in her room—and sometimes her bed—for several days, despite hospital regulations against dogs.

Marianne's 11-year-old sister, Willa, has had rheumatic fever since April and she spent a week in the same hospital room with her.

Mrs. Alexander, whose husband died two years ago, explained Marianne was the youngest of five children.

"We have had a lot of sickness," she said, "I just knew Marianne was going to die. But thanks to the Lord, the doctor and my baby's fighting spirit, she is getting well!"

Willa's wedding picture: From L to R, Hugh, mother, Smith, Willa's husband, Willa, Marianne, Sara, and Lea.

Hugh Causey Alexander, Senior,
with his puppy.

Hugh Causey Alexander, Senior,
at 18 years old.

Annie and Causey's wedding.

Grandfather Evans.

Evans Family.

Evans Family: The couple on the lower right are Annie and Causey.

Dining room, Magruder house.

Living room, Magruder house.

Living room, Magruder house.

The Magruder house.

Polly the horse.

Hugh

Hugh

Hugh

Hugh Causey Alexander, Jr., Magruder house.

Hugh on seesaw.

Hugh, Willa, and Lea in pony cart at Magruder house.

Aunt Minnie and Uncle Billy.

Aunt Sally and Uncle Jule.

Marianne on the 150-year-old, four-poster bed
which has been passed down in the family.

Made in the USA
Lexington, KY
21 October 2017